Teens with Autism

Apps, Ideas for Lessons, & Common Core Reading Connections for Teens and Young Adults with Autism and Developmental Delays

By: S.B. Linton

© 2013 by S. B. Linton. www.autismclassroom.com

All rights reserved.

This book may not be reproduced, stored in a retrieval system, or transmitted by any means electronic, mechanical, photocopying, recording, or otherwise, without written permission from the author.

First Edition: July 2013

Table of Contents

Page 4...The Color Wheel

Page 8...Arithmetic and Geometry

Page 12...Getting to Know Me

Page 16...The Four Seasons

Page 20...The World of Work

Page 24...On the Move/Community Fun

Page 28...Common Core Reading & Language Arts Connections

Page 37...Mobile Apps

Page 50...Notes

Page 51...Resources

Kingsville Public Library
6006 Academy Street
Kingsville, OH 44048-0057

The Color Wheel

Following a Topic/Joint Attention

- Use 3-4 differently colored containers to play desktop "basketball." Ask the students to place the ball in a specific colored container.
- Work cooperatively to compile a mailing together. Use various colored sheets of paper, in a certain order to be placed in the envelope.
- Play catch with baseballs of various colors and mitts of various colors. Ask for a specific color to be thrown or thrown to.

Visual and Performing Arts

- Using sign language, have the students perform a poem or song about colors.
- Use oil pastels to create beautiful works of art. Start with a central black construction paper image glued to white paper. Then have the students use the colorful oil pastels to fill in the rest of the paper. Frame the art work on a piece of black construction paper.
- Create an abstract piece of art by making a ceramic or clay vase. Pick a color to paint it after it dries.

Communication

- Talk about Race Cars and Monster Trucks. Show several pictures. Have students identify the various colors on the logos of the vehicles. Ask students to bring in their own toy cars or trucks to race in a classroom "Grand Prix." Create a sand pit/dirt pit to race the trucks and a long road to race the cars.
- Make a food pyramid on large chart paper. Ask students to request the food picture they would like to glue on the food pyramid. Have each student glue on pictures of various foods in the appropriate places on the food pyramid.

- Use student suggestions for favorite activities to create a class logo for your room. Have each student point to or tell you one of their favorite activities to include in the logo.

Health/Daily Living Skills

- Talk about fiction vs. non-fiction books. Remind students of a silly book they read when they were younger called *Green Eggs and Ham*. Make green eggs using a task analysis with pictures as directions.
- Practice reading and locating household items in a store circular. Then cut out products from the store circular and sort them by the color of the package.
- Teach students a self-monitoring system that incorporates colors to express various emotional states.

Vocational Skills

- For a few days, have students practice matching place settings on a color-coded teacher-made placemat. Then ask them to set the table independently for a "special" lunch.
- Sort classroom laundry or bring in some "laundry" to sort by color.
- Have an on-the-go color match. Bring in "paint chip" cards from a hardware store to start. Give each student 2 cards to find. Have students go to the hardware store and search the paint samples section to find a similar "paint chip" card.

Social Skills

- Have students practice complimenting each other based on the color of their clothing or the color of an item on their desk.
- Study the color spectrum wheel. Then have students create a group project about the color wheel and about opposite colors.
- Play Dominos™, with color coded Dominos.

Recreational Activities (model for the students and play with them)

- Play the game Twister™ or a modified version.
- Have students become architects. Build a house with colored popcicle sticks. (If needed, create a teacher model or framework to have students continue working from.)

- Using a tub or pool of blue tissue paper and magnetic teacher-made fish, have students "fish" using a real fishing rod with a magnet on the end.

Science/Sensory Involvement/STEM

- Investigate using Prisms. Have students use a light source such as the sun, and a prism or mirror and water. Discuss the colors they see as they "investigate."
- Make a mini volcano. Use blue or brown colored sand or clay for the outside and baking soda for the lava. Pour in vinegar (with red food coloring in it) and watch it explode.
- Conduct a paper chromatography experiment. Use a clear container, a tiny sponge, a coffee filter, non-permanent markers and water to separate colors. Folder the coffee filters into a cone like shape. Color the coffee filter at the tip of the cone. Place the tip into the clear container that has the small amount of water on the tiny sponge and watch the colors from the marker separate.

Social Studies (History, Geography, Government)

- Have students locate their favorite flag or the flag of their home country. Make a replica on construction paper. Talk about the colors in each person's flag.
- Look for Rainforest animals with vivid colors. Have students pick their favorite top 10 rainforest animals. Use their choices to create a Powerpoint™ presentation showing various animals with bright colors.
- Locate an image of the state flag for your state or a random state. Mix food coloring into icing and decorate sugar cookies with various colors. Have students purposefully plan which colors to mix based on the colors in the flag of the state they are studying.

Literacy Skills

- Look through magazines to find red items. Have students verbalize or use a voice output device to help non-verbal students participate. Show the flash card for the written word red. Using one distracter, have students match the written word to a flash card. Repeat for various colors.

- Use ribbons to do a "color guard" presentation. Work with the color guard in the school to have a peer design and teach a color guard routine to the class. Use large cue cards to show "up," "down," "left," "right" and "around."
- Eat the colors of the rainbow. Match a food item up to the teacher-made rainbow or color wheel. Then have students request each item based on color. Using a communication board with pictures, have each student comment on the taste (bitter, sour, sweet, bland.)

Fine Motor

- Build a model car together.
- Play Connect Four™ to work on using a pincer grasp.
- Play the game KerPlunk™ to work on using fine motor skills.

Physical Education

- Discuss the colors black and white. Play soccer with a black and white soccer ball.
- Travel the school on a treasure hunt for colors. Give each student a checklist with the colors to look for and have them hold it in their hand so that they will know what to search for. Have them check off the color as they locate it.
- Have Potato sack (or pillowcase) race. Before the race help each student to tie-dye their potato sack or pillow case their favorite color.

Arithmetic & Geometry

Following a Topic/Joint Attention

- Fill a clear container with water then add food coloring. Discuss the concept of volume. Practice using a liquid measuring cup to add a specific amount.
- Make a paper airplane, a model rocket or bring in a toy rocket or battery operated helicopter. Have students count down to a fun blastoff.
- Make an auditory pattern using pretend cymbals (quiet cymbals) such as paper plates, cardstock paper, paper fans, etc. Model the pattern and have the students follow your movements.

Visual and Performing Arts

- Have students make artistic number art drawings by placing a flat number (related to the weekly theme) under white paper and coloring over the paper to see the design.
- Perform a hip-hop or pop dance to a song with numbers in the chorus.
- Make abstract drawings using geometric shapes on a computer based program.

Communication

- Make a pretend restaurant in the classroom. Create a menu with prices. Give students money to practice paying the correct amount for the food item they want to purchase. Have students communicate the items they would like to buy by pointing or using words.
- Make a monthly calendar for events that occur at school or at home. Have students indicate each day when special events will occur.

- Teach students to communicate their expectations (ex. " I think it will...") and predictions about an upcoming experiment. Chart the predictions, then complete the experiment.

Health/Daily Living Skills

- Use a picture board with a numbered recipe (ex. 1 marshmallow, 2 raisins, 3 apple slices, etc.) to make a food "party mix" in a bowl. Give each student a numbered picture cart with the number of each food they need to prepare the mix.
- Have students compare digital clock times and face clock times to schedules in the TV guide for their favorite shows.
- View the back of the box's nutrition label before making popcorn. Count how many calories, fat grams and carbohydrates are in it. Compare it to a lower fat brand. Eat both!

Vocational Skills

- Sort and collate several stacks of paper for a school wide mailing. Make each pile have its own number. Have students compile according to the number.
- Practice using a calculator to add sums on an actual grocery list (using a store advertisement.)
- Set up a store in the classroom. Use real coins and dollar bills to have students buy items from the store.

Social Skills

- Using a picture board with information about the topic, practice taking 3 communication exchanges during a teacher-led conversation.
- Use jellybeans of different colors to practice making patterns. Incorporate models for the students to copy as well as "open" patterns for them to complete. Ask students work as a team to complete the task.
- With a peer from the class or from a social skills group, have the student play the card game "War."

Recreational Skills (Model for the students and play with them)

- Using the computer or a mobile device, play a game similar to Tetris.™

- Use Tangrams™ or a similar toy to increase proficiency in making geometric configurations.
- Use Uno™ Cards to play a modified card game.

Science/Sensory Involvement/STEM

- Use ceramic clay to make a ceramic image/sculpture of a number.
- Measure items to make "slime." Use 1 teaspoon of soluble fiber, 1 cup of water, food coloring and directions from an internet search for "slime."
- Predict the distance between one place in the school and another. Measure the distance between both places to see if the prediction was correct.

Social Studies (History, Geography, Government)

- Measure the longitude and latitude of various places on a globe. Use a string to have students predict the distance from a certain point, then measure the distance together.
- Create a pattern of a map of the world with shapes, using felt or card stock paper. Have the students fill in the missing pieces while highlighting the names of the continents and countries.
- Discuss ancient cultures and then the Roman culture. Look at ancient calligraphy and writings of roman numerals. Have students recreate the roman numerals or match the roman numerals to the actual number.

Literacy Skills

- Teach students to enter data on a computer. Have them spell number words on a computer keyboard. Use a sheet of paper with the number to be typed as a guide.
- Have students present a presentation about their top 3 favorite things. Ask them to highlight what is first, second and third. Using powerpoint or a science board, chart paper or poster board, they can present to the group (using words, signs, voice output devices or pictures.) Have students sequence a story using three squares labeled "first," "second," and "third."
- Identify coins or add coins to make various sums.

Fine Motor

- Try Origami.
- Practice sending a text message.
- Play a game on a mobile device.

Physical Education

- Raise money for a good cause by having your own 5-K walk/run or 1-mile walk/run. Set the distance using large number markers to mark each foot, yard or meter they walk/run. Involve the whole school community.
- Emphasize the shapes found throughout the game of baseball or T-ball. Create your own diamond and play a game of baseball or t-ball with another class.
- Have a long jump competition. Measure the distance of each person's jump.

Getting to Know Me

Following a Topic/Joint Attention

- Ask students to bring in pictures of family members at a recent family activity, with details of the event (written on the back from mom or dad) and look at the pictures with the student while reading the details of what occurred.
- Look through a magazine or brochure of the individual's favorite toys, books or character.
- Make a textured bag filled with materials or items related to a recent community trip, a fun school activity or a "trip" around the school building. Have the students take turns reaching inside and pulling out a textured item and commenting on it.

Visual and Performing Arts

- Study/teach the term "personification." Then have the students pretend to be a tree with falling leaves or have them act out other inanimate objects.
- Use colored pencils and a sketch pad to make self-portraits together.
- Have the students make a diorama box of their classroom or home.

Communication

- Have students and parents make a visual art project about their summer vacation. Have each student share what they made. Ask parents to send in an index card with the written details of the summer vacation for the project.
- Make invitations for another class and the office staff members to attend a talent show given by your students. Encourage the students to highlight a talent that they have at the classroom talent show. Be creative to make sure that all students participate.
- Have an "art show" in your room. Invite parents and the principal. Have the students communicate their information about their works of art using

words or by holding up a large sign with their name, project title and details.

Health/Daily Living Skills

- Practice the procedure for various activities that occur throughout the day. Show the students the expectations of each activity. Make a video to model the specific skills you want the students to learn. Show the video, then, re-practice the skill.
- Create a visual cookbook of cooking recipes that each student creates. Compile the recipes and visual pictures and give the book as a gift to parents at holiday time or for the summer.
- Have students make a gift for family members to say thank you to loved ones. Have them place the gift in a box, then, practice wrapping by using tissue paper or construction paper.

Vocational Skills

- Give out weekly, meaningful classroom jobs and hold students accountable for completing their job. Practice the expectations of each job. Make a board with a picture of each job and of each student's name. Have them check-in when it is time to complete the job and check-out when they are done.
- Have a variety of locks and keys. Have students match the keys to the locks to open the locks.
- Discuss recycling. Take a tour of the school to locate recycling bins. As a class, collect the recycled items and bag them together to go to their final destination. Consult with the custodian about the best way to collaborate on this activity.

Social Skills

- Write a book with each student called "My Favorite Things." Ask them to share the book with their family when the book is completed.
- Practice greeting office staff members by taking a trip to the office one by one. Make the greeting based on the communication level of the student. As the year progresses, require more and more advanced communication skills.

- Use role play and video modeling to talk about personal space and respecting other's personal space. Have students and peers act out appropriate vs. inappropriate ways to deal with personal space.

Recreational Skills (Model for the students and play with them)

- Talk about occupations that students may have an interest in pursuing. Discuss the field of medicine. Pretend to be surgeons and play the game Operation™.
- Do a group line dance together in which all members of the group do the same dance moves.
- Play modified tennis by hitting the ball against a wall.

Science/Sensory Involvement/STEM

- Create a sensory profile for each student with help from the Occupational Therapist. Use this information to create a classroom that is sensitive to the sensory needs of teens.
- Go outside with each student and have them collect their favorite flowers, then have them arrange a bouquet for the principal and office staff.
- Use jewelry making craft materials and fake gems to make a necklace or bracelet. In the summer, use twine and beads to make a "surfer's" wrist band.

Social Studies (History, Geography, Government)

- Have an international food tasting day where the students taste foods, then try to identify which country the food originated.
- Create a graph of students who have siblings. Count how many students have brothers and how many have sisters and how many have both brothers and sisters.
- Work with the students to search the internet to find information about a family from a specific time period.

Literacy Skills

- Read a comic book together for fun.
- Use the computer to have students practice typing their own names and filling out a form or application.

- Ask students to bring in baby pictures. Have a photo "contest" to see what school team members can match the baby pictures to the student's picture today.

Fine Motor

- Emphasize the letters in their first name. Have students identify a picture of themselves. Use pipe cleaners to make the letters of their name.
- Practice lacing and tying shoes using colorful shoelaces.
- Create a family tree for each student using pictures or photo copies of pictures sent in from home. Have students label the person's name using calligraphy or by tracing calligraphy.

Physical Education

- Toss and catch with a lacrosse stick.
- Make up drills with a basketball. Have students complete the drills.
- Play flag football. Ask students to wear their favorite team's jersey.

The Four Seasons

Following a Topic/Joint Attention

- Read or look through a vacation brochure together and talk about the summer activities shown in the brochure.
- Have a snowball fight. Use real snow or fake snow together.
- Practice calling relatives to make holiday greetings. Use a script, while you pretend to make phone call together to a relative to wish them a happy holiday season.

Visual and Performing Arts

- Play the "follow the singer" game. Sing group Karaoke and have the "crowd' sing along with the person who has the microphone.
- Sing Karaoke with seasonal songs that have gestures that accompany them. Have the students imitate the gestures and the silly sounds in the songs.
- Have the students imitate you as you are "conducting" an orchestra, while listening to classical music.

Communication

- Have students identify their favorite thing about the current season using magazine cut outs, pictures and icons. Use their ideas to help them create a letter home to their family about their favorite seasonal things.
- Use a fan and various sized objects. Ask students to make a prediction about the force of the wind from the fan. Have them tell you which item they think will move the farthest based on its weight and size.
- Have students write a letter to a family member or pen pal and mail it in a mailbox or mail it on a trip to the post office.

Health/Daily Living Skills

- Build a birdhouse together using picture directions.
- Rake fall leaves or shovel snow in the winter.
- Use crushed ice, fruit and other seasonal ingredients to make a smoothie fit for the season.

Vocational Skills

- Use a variety of brochures from vacation spots to have students determine if the brochures depict traditional winter, spring, summer or autumn activities.
- Practice using a stapler to staple the top of an envelope filled with planting seeds. Decorate the envelope. Have students give the seeds as a gift to a favorite faculty member. Or use the packets of seeds for a fund raiser.
- Practice packing a backpack for a camping trip or a vacation. Set out the items in a specific order and give the students a numbered checklist (with photos) to follow. Encourage students to independently read the checklist and pack the backpack.

Social Skills

- Have a beach party or winter wonderland with another class. Have students create all of the decorations. During the party, practice learned skills related to group gatherings.
- Role-play visiting family and friend for summer vacation. Teach the students some phrases they could say or some situations they might encounter while on vacation.
- Discuss migration and hibernation. Make a chart with a column for each word. Have students ask other students where to place the picture. Have them place pictures of 10 animals in the appropriate category for which animal migrates and which animal hibernates during the winter.

Recreational Skills (Model for the students and play with them)

- Use a water bottle to spray in the air and make a spring shower.
- Pretend to be a boxer in training. Complete a kick boxing workout or any other work out that a boxer might use.
- Go for a jog.

Science/Sensory Involvement/STEM

- Identify scents of the season with eyes closed or blindfolds.
- Visit a pet store or aquarium, then, create an aquarium in the classroom using direct input from each of the students.
- Have a water balloon toss (over-hand) while predicting the distance the balloons will go based on their size and weight.

Social Studies (History, Geography, Government)

- Plant seasonal "crops" after visiting a farmers market.
- Study farming cultures. Watch a video about teens in a culture different than your own.
- Read the phone book or search the internet to locate fun activities for young adults and for visitors in your area.

Literacy Skills

- Use sentence strips to have students retell a story about a recent event or party.
- Make a seasonal collage that spells the name of the season. Fill it in with items observed in that season.
- Discuss various winter holiday traditions. Practice "sharing" as friends and family do at Kwanzaa. Emphasize the word "share" as the students pass around a highly motivating item or food tray/bowl.

Fine Motor

- Hide seasonal items and items of high interest to teenagers, in a various zippered baggies and closed containers. Have students use fine motor skills to open the items.
- Create a memorable keepsake ornament using ceramic circles from a craft store and artist's paint.
- Make various crafts to wear and use at a New Years' Eve Party. Have students decorate their items and noise makers to take home for their own family celebration.

Physical Education

- Study the armed forces and what they do for the citizens of the world. Discuss the idea of a "boot camp." Set up a spring "boot camp" and have the students exercise outside to encourage physical fitness.
- Make your own beach scene and play beach volleyball.
- Hold a Winter Olympics training camp for the students. Have each student choose a sport to learn about and practice. Give each student an opportunity to show off the basic rules or moves related to that sport.

The World of Work

Following a Topic/Joint Attention

- Read a grocery store circular to make a shopping list. Look through the circular together to have each student choose the items they would like to buy at the store.
- Have students play the role of a party planner to plan a party for the class. Include a water balloon toss and other fun games that occur at parties.
- Visit a florist or have students go online to see what a florist does. Ask students to work together to make a flower garden or a special bouquet for someone (using either real flowers or using construction paper and tissue paper flowers.)

Communication

- Teach students to read body language. Play the game of Charades to have them look for clues about what a person is trying to portray without using words.
- Encourage self-advocacy by teaching students to ask for "help." Provide a "help" sign and teach students the appropriate time to use it.
- Make boards or sheets of paper with photos, words or icons about a topic. Teach the students to use that board to point to pictures to talk about the topic.

Visual and Performing Arts

- Be a "commissioned artist" for the day. Use a large white sheet and paint to make a class mural.
- Have the students create a graphic design to promote the book you are reading for the week.
- Choose from pictures of several people at various jobs. Have students act out what that person may do while at work.

Health/Daily Living Skills

- Conduct an interest inventory to see what careers students have an interest in pursuing. Search the internet to find an inventory tool that is appropriate for the student's developmental level and reading level. Create your own, using pictures, if needed.
- Play a game in which students have to match clothing to the appropriate situation (ex. Relaxing at home vs. job interview or going to the movies vs. visiting the president.)
- Go to a bank or create a bank in the classroom. Have students count out their money, then fill out deposit slips with the correct amount of cash/coins and hand it to the teller (or teacher).

Vocational Skills

- Encourage productivity by giving students a picture schedule with 3 or more easy, hands-on (non-worksheets) tasks or jobs. Encourage them to manipulate the schedule themselves to complete the tasks in sequential order. Give only gesture prompts to help them finish.
- Conduct an activity with messy materials that you may not normally do because of the mess. Have students use a broom or vacuum to encourage students to clean up after themselves.
- Use a basket and bookshelf to have students practice shelving books. Give the students the books in a basket and have them either shelve randomly or have them shelve by name, color, etc.

Social Skills

- Have lunch with peers and practice discussing pop culture topics that teens talk about.
- Read a magazine such as *News-2-You* or *The Social Times* to build knowledge about current events and social skills.
- Work as a team to make a project by giving each student a significant part of the project to complete. Practice developing teamwork skills that are needed for the work world.

Recreational Activities

- Learn about zoologists. Take a trip to the zoo. Have students interview a zookeeper.
- Build structures using K-nex™.
- Read through fashion magazines to discuss the career of a fashion designer.

Science/Sensory Involvement/STEM

- Be engineers. Draw out a plan for a large building, then use large cardboard boxes to construct the building.
- Study some topics in exercise science. Practice several relaxation techniques to calm and relax such as meditation and yoga. Add visual supports, videos, music, and timers to help students be successful in implementing the techniques.
- Talk to students about how they might pack a nutritious sensory lunch for "work." Using the food pyramid, try to make a meal that has smells, tastes, textures and "sounds" and is healthy.

Social Studies (History, Geography, Government)

- Read or highlight topics from a book about the industrial revolution. Have students take turns using some items that were created during that period of time.
- Present the students with information about various cities in the world that may relate to whatever theme you are presenting. Have the students make a sign or poster of that city with pictures or objects of exciting things to do in that city.
- Read a story book that has a moral related to working hard. Ask students to study the work habits of the characters in the story by creating a visual story board that highlights work traits that are positive and work traits that are undesirable.

Literacy Skills

- Play telling time bingo. Make a teacher-made board with time by the hour, half-hour or by 15 minute increments. Have students match a bingo marker on their board if they have the number you call, when you hold up a card.

- Match definitions of work related words to the words using index cards.
- Read a book about a going to work or make a story about this topic. Make a collage about things to do at work.

Fine Motor

- Have students use a hole punch to "punch tickets" as students arrive at an upcoming school event.
- Practice signing a signature at the bottom of a page.
- Practice entering appointments or assignments on a calendar. Use an actual calendar and a digital calendar.

Physical Education

- Have a 40 yard dash.
- Play golf.
- Roller skate.

On the Move/ Community Fun

Following a Topic/Joint Attention

- Make a model airplane and fly it in the air. Watch it fly together.
- Fly a kite together.
- Play "wall ball" by using a tennis ball and throwing the ball against a solid wall, then catching it.

Visual and Performing Arts

- Go to an art museum to see abstract or make art with magnets (under the paper), paint (on top of the paper), paper and a metal object (on top of the paper).
- Go to a free an outdoor concert or watch the school band practice.
- Dance. Listen to popular songs and have a class dance or party with another classroom.

Communication

- Ask each student to express (through words or pictures) their favorite mode of transportation. Graph each student's response. Have the student interpret the graph.
- Visit several community helpers. Have students interview the community helper. Use words, pictures or symbols to help students ask their questions. Before going, practice the script for the interview.
- Encourage conversation skills using a highly favored TV show or item. Begin by showing a picture first, then starting the conversation. Use words, pictures or symbols on a paper to help students communicate. Teach conversation skills by teaching students to take turns in the conversation and to stay engaged in a conversation until the conversation has ended.

Health/Daily Living Skills

- Have students choose a song they want to exercise to. Exercise.
- Teach students the "rules of the road" and the rules for pedestrians using transportation signs. Act out a scene of how to cross the street or watch video modeling of the correct way to walk at a cross walk.
- Teach the meaning of 911 and practice making the call for future reference. Use a script to tell the information that the 911 operator will ask (ex. address, phone number, etc.)

Vocational Skills

- Take a ride on public transportation or take a ride on a train. Have the students read the bus schedule ahead of time and complete the payment transaction independently.
- Identify various types of signs that mean "men's bathroom," "women's bathroom" and "family bathroom." Teach the students which bathroom is suitable for them.
- Go to a pet store or an animal shelter and volunteer for the day or for an hour. Ask the vet or store manager if one or several students can help them groom a pet.

Social Skills

- Teach the students to ask for help or to locate a security guard or police officer when out in the community. Play a matching game to locate community helpers in uniform.
- Have a weekly video game party with peers or family members of the same age. Coach peers on autism awareness and respect for differences. Teach peers ways to invite students into conversations, stand up against bullying, and encourage turn taking while playing the video games.
- Ask students to create a picture story about a community helper that they like the best. Have them share their story (by pointing to the pictures or by speaking) with a family member when the final product is sent home. Highlight several items that they must cover when presenting to their family or several questions the family member must ask them.

Recreational Skills (Model for the students and play with them)

- Go outside and play a game of Frisbee.
- Teach students to play the game of Horseshoes.
- Create a buddy group of peers from other members of the school environment. Have the members of the group practice tennis together or bowling. Sponsor a monthly on bi-monthly community outing to a tennis court or a bowling alley.

Science/Sensory Involvement/STEM

- Be scientist and mix elements together to make scented dough. Wear goggles and lab coats.
- Use black paper to create a scene of the universe. Try getting some paint and glitter glue that glows in the dark.
- Pretend to parasail or parachute by putting on the gear and taking turns jumping from a step stool.

Social Studies (History, Geography, Politics)

- Make a pretend passport using construction paper, glue, and a photo.
- Use the internet to "travel" to various countries. Stamp the student's passports as they "visit" each county.
- Visit the school library to see books about the countries the students "traveled" to.

Literacy Skills

- Show the students words they may see when out and about. Have them practice indentifying the words. Complete a worksheet matching the word to the picture of the item.
- Practice reading a map of the school. Go on a "treasure hunt" for 1 or 2 specific things. Use the map to travel to the location of those things.
- Get a map of the USA. Show student the various states and capitals. Have students express (words, signs or pictures) which state they like the best. Print out the name of your state capital. Have them match the state capital of your state with the state, on a worksheet.

Fine Motor

- Have a Tug of War Contest.
- Crumple up paper to shoot into a wastebasket. Have a contest.
- Cut coupons for your next class shopping trip.

Physical Education
- Take the students to the workout room or gym. Have peers as coaches and ask the peers to develop a fitness routine to implement once a week or more.
- Use a stopwatch or another unit of measurement to track time or distance when taking a walk. Allow students access to their MP3 music, if available. Log your distance each time after finishing. Work toward a reward when you hit a milestone.
- Make a balancing activity using string on the floor or tape on the floor. Have students walk on the line from one point to another without stepping off of the tape or string.

Common Core Connections for Reading

Currently, many states are adopting the Common Core as their primary curriculum guide. Many Special Educators wonder what this will mean for students receiving special education services since the Common Core needs to be followed and student learning still needs to be individualized. The following ideas are for students with autism or with intellectual disabilities in grades 6-12. The suggestions are ideas on how to make the common core reading standards more accessible to students with autism or with intellectual disabilities. A practical example, which can be modified according to the learner's needs, is presented for each standard.

Literacy Anchor 1: *Read closely to determine what the text says explicitly and to make logical inferences from it; cite specific textual evidence when writing or speaking to support conclusions drawn from the text.*

- Read a book or story. Ask students to complete a worksheet that allows them to use photos and pre-written index cards to fill in the blanks. Have them choose between two choices to pick the answer that correctly finishes the sentence. For example, "_____ is sad because he said _____." or "Sammy is _____ because _____."

Literacy Anchor 2: *Determine central ideas or themes of a text and analyze their development; summarize the key supporting details and ideas.*

- Read a short story or book. Use sentence strips and pre-written word cards to create a summary of the story. Have students fill in the pre-written word cards in the correct blank areas to create the summary of the story.

Literacy Anchor 3: *Analyze how and why individuals, events, or ideas develop and interact over the course of a text.*

- Read a book about a character that transforms during the story. Create a beginning, middle and end graph to show the differences in the character at the beginning, middle and end of the story. Try dividing the paper into 3 sections which say "Beginning. Middle. End."

Literacy Anchor 4: *Interpret words and phrases as they are used in a text, including determining technical, connotative, and figurative meanings, and analyze how specific word choices shape meaning or tone.*

- Discover the world of pirates through videos and various books. Analyze 5 popular pirate phrases while discussing the language of pirates with the students. Use real pictures to show the feelings associated with the tone of each word.

Literacy Anchor 5: *Analyze the structure of texts, including how specific sentences, paragraphs, and larger portions of the text (e.g., a section, chapter, scene, or stanza) relate to each other and the whole.*

- Read a short cooking recipe. Discuss how the numbered sequences relate to each other and that they work together to make an entire product at the end. Have each recipe direction on a sentence strip and place them out of order. Ask students their thoughts on the end product with the jumbled instructions. Then, have them re-order the recipe instructions in the correct order using a visual model of the original recipe.

Literacy Anchor 6: *Assess how point of view or purpose shapes the content and style of a text.*

- Show students a paragraph or newspaper article about a local amusement park or fun activity center. Then show them a brochure about the same amusement park or activity center. Discuss the purpose of both. Discuss the style of each. Compare the two styles.

As a class, make a paragraph about a fictional amusement park. Have each student create a fictional brochure about the fictional amusement park.

Literacy Anchor 7: *Integrate and evaluate content presented in diverse media and formats, including visually and quantitatively, as well as in words.*

- Using a teacher written list, have the students practice reading and locating household items in the store circular. Next, have the students make a grocery list by cutting out the pictures and pasting them on their own list. Use the list at the next grocery store trip.

Literacy Anchor 8: *Delineate and evaluate the argument and specific claims in a text, including the validity of the reasoning as well as the relevance and sufficiency of the evidence.*

- Read a teens magazine article about the upcoming holiday. Use the text to tell what colors are associated with the holiday, when the holiday occurs and what people do on that holiday.

Literacy Anchor 9: *Analyze how two or more texts address similar themes or topics in order to build knowledge or to compare the approaches the authors take.*

- Use a graphic organizer such as a Venn diagram to compare prices in various store circulars for 6 items. Use cut out pictures of food items to place on the Venn diagram while comparing prices from various stores.

Literacy Anchor 10: *Read and comprehend complex literary and informational texts independently and proficiently.*

- Have students attempt to independently read a recipe color-coded, task analysis (with whole number measurements of ingredients) to create a 6 ingredient meal or snack based on colors. For example, 1 cup of oranges, 2 cups of yellow bananas, three cups of green grapes.

Writing Anchor 1: *Write arguments to support claims in an analysis of substantive topics or texts using valid reasoning and relevant and sufficient evidence.*

- Use the computer to locate a current event story or use a kid's magazine borrowed from the public library. Post a question that asks "What are the 2 major points of the story?" Using written words or pictures, have students fill in the blanks on a worksheet or magnetic board to complete the sentence " _____is _____because_____."

Writing Anchor 2: *Write informative/explanatory texts to examine and convey complex ideas and information clearly and accurately through the effective selection, organization, and analysis of content.*

- View a book with photos or look at online photos of monster trucks or sports cars. Have students make or color a replica of their favorite car or truck logo. Help them to create a poster board presentation that shows the logo, a picture of the car or truck, the place the car is made and a few fun facts about the car or truck. Allow them to share it with their peers in a show and tell format. Use pre-recorded voice output devices for non-speakers.

Writing Anchor 3: *Write narratives to develop real or imagined experiences or events using effective technique, well-chosen details and well-structured event sequences.*

- Have students complete a paragraph to send home to their parents. Use the student's personalized schedule and a teacher-made template to review the activities from the school day. The students can fill in pictures or words after leading sentences such as "First we_____. Next we_____. Then we_____. After that, at school we_____."

Writing Anchor 4: *Produce clear and coherent writing in which the development, organization, and style are appropriate to task, purpose, and audience.*

- Identify a favorite product or a product that your class has found particularly helpful. Have each student write a business letter using words and fill in the blank spaces to tell the company how much they liked the product. Help them by allowing pre-chosen picture icons or pre-chosen words to fill in the blanks spaces. Or, write a letter to the principal using this same format.

Writing Anchor 5: *Develop and strengthen writing as needed by planning, revising, editing, rewriting, or trying a new approach.*

- Visit the library and get books about the chemistry of the color wheel and how paints mix together to make new paint colors. Visit a hardware store to look at paint and watch them mix paint colors. As a group, make a list of 3 things you liked about visiting. Use the list to create a draft letter on the board or on chart paper. (Include 4 misspellings and punctuation mistakes.) As a group, edit and revise the letter that will be sent to the hardware store.

Writing Anchor 6: *Use technology, including the Internet, to produce and publish writing and to interact and collaborate with others.*

- Using the computer and an internet search of images, view pictures of people in Medieval Times. Read a short article about the history of Medieval Times and the use of shields of armor. Have students make personal shields of armor. Or make one large shield as a group, for the class. Together, decide what words will go on the shield.

Writing Anchor 7: *Conduct short as well as more sustained research projects based on focused questions, demonstrating understanding of the subject under investigation.*

- Set up a polling booth. Run an election for favorite color of the year. Be sure to include the age, grade, and whether the voter is a boy or girl on the ballot so that the class can interpret the results using various measures.

Writing Anchor 8: *Gather relevant information from multiple print and digital sources, assess the credibility and accuracy of each source, and integrate the information while avoiding plagiarism.*

- Get a DK Eyewitness book about a topic of your choosing. Use the internet search engine images and a kids magazine from the library with information about the topic. Make a classroom bulletin board about the topic. Use various sources to answer the questions "What is it?," "Why is it important?" and "What does it look like?" Make a poster for each question and hang them onto the bulletin board.

Writing Anchor 9: *Draw evidence from literary or informational texts to support analysis, reflection, and research.*

- Choose a favorite video game. Teach the students how to read the game directions to learn how to play the video game. Or teach them how to read instructions that tell how to move to the next level on the game.

Writing Anchor 10: *Write routinely over extended time frames (time for research, reflection, and revision) and shorter time frames (a single sitting or a day or two) for a range of tasks, purposes, and audiences.*

- Ask students to practice typing their name, address and phone number into the computer. Give a visual template to them to refer to when typing.

Speaking and Listening Anchor 1: *Prepare for and participate effectively in a range of conversations and collaborations with diverse partners, building on others' ideas and expressing their own clearly and persuasively.*

- Ask students to take a look around and notice what colors and patterns others are wearing. Have students use a visual topic board with pictures and colored-in spaces to point to their answers about what a specific student is wearing. Afterward, ask each student to share their favorite color by holding up a large piece of construction paper with that color on it.

Speaking and Listening Anchor 2: *Integrate and evaluate information presented in diverse media and formats, including visually, quantitatively, and orally.*

- Conduct a science experiment related to mixing colors. Have each student present what they came up with after they mixed their two colors. Use construction paper with pre-written spaces, two boxes for "start" and one box for "finish." Ask students to place picture icons of the colors in the blank spaces. At the bottom of the paper have a fill-in the blank sentence that says "I mixed ____ and ___ and now it is___."

Speaking and Listening Anchor 3: *Evaluate a speaker's point of view, reasoning, and use of evidence and rhetoric.*

- View the "I Have Dream" speech. Answer these questions with the students: What was the topic?, How did he feel?, How do you know?, Do you have a dream?

Speaking and Listening Anchor 4: *Present information, findings, and supporting evidence such that listeners can follow the line of reasoning and the organization, development, and style are appropriate to task, purpose, and audience.*

- Conduct a science experiment. Give students choices to point to so they can tell their hypothesis. Be sure to write on the board the hypothesis, the steps of the experiment and the actual outcome. Allow students to actively participate in the experiment.

Speaking and Listening Anchor 5: *Make strategic use of digital media and visual displays of data to express information and enhance understanding of presentations.*

- Have students create a piece of collage art using their favorite color, shape or sport. Encourage the students to find 5 pictures of the topic from various sources. One from the computer, 1 actual photo, 1 from a newspaper, 2 from a magazine and 1 student created drawing.

Speaking and Listening Anchor 6: *Adapt speech to a variety of contexts and communicative tasks, demonstrating command of formal English when indicated or appropriate.*

- Have a party in the classroom with fun foods that the students like. Have students communicate to get the items. Use pictures, words, icons or voice output devices to encourage communication.

Language Anchor 1: *Demonstrate command of the conventions of standard English grammar and usage when writing or speaking.*

- Use the SentenceBuilder (Mobile Education Store) App to have students create sentences. Practice reading the sentences with the students. If possible, have the students copy the sentence on the app onto paper.

Language Anchor 2: *Demonstrate command of the conventions of standard English capitalization, punctuation, and spelling when writing.*

- On the board or on a large chart paper, create a teacher written paragraph with the input of the students. Choose a topic and write 5 sentences. Have a visual topic board with pictures or phrases for each student to use to point to words or phrases they want added to the paragraph.

Language Anchor 3: *Apply knowledge of language to understand how language functions in different contexts, to make effective choices for meaning or style, and to comprehend more fully when reading or listening.*

- For a multi-day project, have students make a poster-sized family tree with names and pictures. When completed, have students show their poster to the class. Next, have students review the poster of a friend and answer these questions: "Who is _____'s Mom?," Who is ___" Dad?" How many brothers and sisters do they have?" and "How do you know?"

Language Anchor 4: *Determine or clarify the meaning of unknown and multiple-meaning words and phrases by using context clues, analyzing* *meaningful word parts, and consulting general and specialized reference materials, as appropriate.*

- On large chart paper, make a list of words that have multiple meanings and have the students discuss the meanings. Start with the words blue, yellow, green and red.

Language Anchor 5: *Demonstrate understanding of figurative language, word relationships, and nuances in word meanings.*

- Examine the emotions associated with color words. Find a series of pictures to have students match with the color word and pictured emotion for blue, green and red.

Language Anchor 6: *Acquire and use accurately a range of general academic and domain-specific words and phrases sufficient for reading, writing, speaking, and listening at the college and career readiness level; demonstrate independence in gathering vocabulary knowledge when encountering an unknown term important to comprehension or expression.*

- Have the students work with the teacher to complete a personal information form, an application for a magazine subscription or a job application template. Use pre-cut word strips to help students who are non-writers to fill in the blanks.

Apps

Recently, mobile apps have become a huge learning tool in the field of education. Even AutismClassroom.com has a series of informational apps (*Autism Classroom, Classroom Set Up, Autism at Home, Teens with Autism & Developmental Delays,* and *Behavior Support for Autism & Special Education*) intended for the professional development and personal development of educators, service providers and parents who want to learn more about teaching children with autism. However, most apps that are created are interactive apps for children. Below are a few apps for the iPad™ and ideas about how they can be incorporated into lessons and activities. Some apps listed below can be purchased in the store for the iPhone™ or iPod Touch™ and then integrated onto the iPad™. Others are for the iPad™ exclusively. Many of the apps offer a free version or a "Lite" version of the app so that you can test it out before purchasing the full version. The bolded type provides the name of the app, the company or developer name and the price of the app at the time of this printing of this publication.

Following a Topic/Joint Attention

- **Fruit Ninja (Half Brick Studios, $0.99)**- Have the student play this app with a peer or a teacher. Practice slicing fruit together and listen to the sound effects on the iPad™.
- **Conversation Coach Lite (Silver Lining Multimedia Inc., $2.99)**- This app can be used to help a student practice staying on topic in a conversation.
- **Spot the Difference (Reign Design, Free)**- Project the image on a large screen for the class. Work as a team to identify variations in the pictures. Use visual skills to have students point to the differences.
- **Let's Create Pottery App (Infinite Dreams, $4.99)**- Build pretend pottery together with the app.
- **Balloon Pops (Joe Scrivers, $0.99)**- Use this app to emphasize attributes as the balloons go from small to big in this app.
- **Random Touch (Joe Scrivers, $0.99)**- Take turns using this app. Try using two cards with "my turn" and "your turn" to encourage turn taking.

- **Beautiful Bubbles (Joe Scrivers, Free)**- Use this app together as a reading activity. Read the words and have the student follow the written directions.
- **Spot the Dot (Ruckus Media Group, $3.99)**- Do an activity in which the student listens to and follows the verbal directions in the app.
- **Touch Switch (Goatella, $4.99)**- Work with the student to choose a video or musical selection together.
- **Bubble Explode (Spooky House Studios LLG, Free)**- Pop bubbles while emphasizing colors with this app. Watch the bubbles explode while moving on to different levels of the game.

Visual and Performing Arts

- **C-Fit Dance (Classroom Fitness, $0.99)**- Choose a dance style to teach the students. Practice the dance using the app. Then do a performance for the administrators in the building.
- **LaDiDa (Khush Inc., $2.99)**- Write a song based on the unit or theme the class is studying. Use visual supports and picture cards to display the song to the students. Sing the song into the app. Play around with various rhythms to make a song for the class.
- **Color My Name (Girl's World Pty. Ltd, $1.99)**- Have the students make a comic image of themselves or a fun picture related to the lesson.
- **Glitteratti (7twenty7 LLC, Free)**- Use this glitter based app to create a picture based on the lesson or unit you are working on.
- **StoryBuilder For iPad (Mobile Education Store LLC, $7.99)**- Have students tap into their creative talents to build a story from 50 distinct storylines and 500 audio clips of questions that guide the narrative. Email recorded stories home to parents.
- **Jigsaw Pro Puzzle (Critical Hit Software, $2.99)**- Practice building visual spatial skills by putting together puzzles in this app.
- **Lego DC Superheros Movie Maker (The LEGO Group, Free)**- Make producers and directors out of students when they create an action packed motion picture with this app. Use a graphic organizer to have students plan what the film will be about and then execute the plan.
- **Lego Creationary (The LEGO Group, Free)**- Guess what the LEGO's are building by selecting the correct answer from the choices. Students must think quickly to beat the clock.
- **Style Studio Fashion Designer (XMG Studio Inc., $0.99)**- Have the

students make new fashion trends using this app which fosters their creativity. Work on identifying colors and articles of clothing while having fun designing.
- **iDoddle2 (Josiah Larson, $0.99)**- Take photos with the iPad then add the student's own personal creative touches with the colors and images from this app.

Communication

- **Yes/No HD (SimplifiedTouch, $3.99)**- Try this app for having students answer basic yes/no questions during reading or literacy lessons.
- **Artix Pix Sample Version (RinnApps, Free)**- Articulation therapy is the key to this app. Therapists and teachers working with this interactive app will be pleased. It is for students who may need extra help with pronouncing words and sounds.
- **Assistive Chat (Assistive Apps, $24.99)**- Try this app during a science or social studies lesson to check for comprehension of the lesson. Use this app with spellers and writers or teach keyboarding skills to non-spellers. On the app, as the sentence is written, the sentence is read aloud through text-to-speech capabilities.
- **My First AAC by Injini (NC Soft, $24.99)**- Improve communication during a group activity or social skills activity using this app. The customizable screen layout can display 2 large icons or 8 smaller icons per category. Various categories can be programmed into the app. It has more than 250 icons organized by category, the choice of a boy or girl voice, and animated icons.
- **See.Touch.Learn. for Ipad (Brain Parade, Free)**- Use this app with a unit on emotions. Use the emotions "library" to create a board or "lesson" within the app in which the student can have a choice of answers based on the questions you create. The app now has the ability to duplicate the "lesson" consecutively so that more than one student in the group can have the chance to answer the same question without beginning the program over.
- **Articulation Station (Little Bee Speech, Free)**- Use this "lite" version of the $49.99 app to target specific speech sounds as well as to practice reading words and to practice identifying pictures.
- **Proloquo2Go (AssistiveWare, $189.99)**- Students can communicate wants and needs during mealtimes, lesson times and play times with this

app that is well known for its full-featured augmentative and alternative communication solution.
- **Alexicom Elements Teen Home (Alexicom Tech LLC, $19.99)**- Encourage choice-making with one of the screens on this app. It has various screens with pictures that the student can tap and hear a voice recording of what is pictured on the screen.
- **Use 2 Talk (Pablo La Roche, $24.99)**- Real photos or pre-made pictures can be used in this app. Create a pretend restaurant in the class and have students practice ordering food using this app.
- **Auditory Work Out (Virtual Speech Center Inc., $19.99)**- Foster receptive language skills by having students follow directions with increasing levels of difficulty in this auditory processing based app.

Health/Daily Living Skills

- **ASD Timer (In the Round Studios, $2.99)**- Practice building independence with time management using this app. Use it to remind students that their time for a favorite reinforcing activity is almost over.
- **TimeTimer (Time Timer LLC, $1.99)**- Allow the Time Timer app to cue students that time is running out for a specific activity or lesson. Students can visually see the red color go away as the time disappears.
- **Stories2Learn (MDR, $13.99)**- Teach independent skills that can be used during a holiday gathering or school celebration, by creating a story to help focus on specific skills you want to see during that gathering or celebration. This app is customizable and you can upload your own pictures.
- **More Pizza! (Maverick Software LLC, $0.99)**- Use the app to practice making pizza. Create a picture task analysis for baking pizza and have the students use a picture task analysis to bake real pizza.
- **Grocery Signs and Words (Conover Company, $0.99)**- Use the app to learn the words associated with a trip to the grocery store. Create index cards with the new vocabulary words on them and have students match the index card to the word on the screen.
- **Coin Math (Recession Apps LLC, Free)**- Count real looking coins on this app as students answer questions about making change, and paying the correct amount for items. Create a treasure box for the classroom and have students pay for items from the box each day.
- **I get...Going to the Grocery Store (I Get It LLC, $2.99)**- Make a

visual schedule on the go with this app to show what the student will do (ex. Get fruit, wait in line, get deli meat, look for cookies, stand in line, check out, etc.) while in the grocery store. The app allows you to use your own photos.

- **Little Match Ups Tell Time (Grasshopper Apps.com, Free)**- Have students match digital times on the app to the face clocks on the app during a lesson on telling time.
- **Coco Dress Up (Linqsoft Ltd, Free)**- Practice identifying items needed for dressing by choosing from over 400 items to dress the fashion friendly character Coco.
- **Math Bingo (ABCya.com, $0.99)**- Play bingo math as a warm-up or transition into a math lesson. Students can use the addition board after choosing a personalized game character.

Vocational Skills

- **Everyday Skills (Ablelink Technologies Inc., $39.99)**- Use this app with a unit on riding the bus or using public transportation. Use the video that demonstrates using public transportation to teach the skill. Show it on the big screen as a movie. Take a trip on a community bus and have students practice paying for the bus ride or set up a pretend bus stop in the classroom and have students practice.
- **Clean Up Category Sorting (Different Roads to Learning, Inc., $1.99)**- Use the app to teach classifying skills. On the app, have students sort items into food, toys or clothes. Next, have students sort real objects into the food pile, toys pile or clothes pile during the group lesson.
- **Chore Pad HD Lite (Nannek, Free)**- Have students self-monitor their own completion of chores in the classroom or on a vocational job site.
- **My Choice Board (Good Karma Applications, Inc., $9.99)**- Use this app as a portable reinforcement chart. Have the students pick an item they will gain access to after their work is completed.
- **Survival Signs and Words (Conover Company, $0.99)**- Make a list of 10 survival words to ask students to locate within the app. Then, have the students match a pre-written definition (on an index card) to each word you name.
- **Count Money Coin Matching (By GrasshopperApps.com, Free)**- Match various sums of money on the app. Have students practice counting out sums of money to "pay." Take students to the vending

machine or the school store to pay for real items using coins.
- **Everyday Social Skills HD (Conover Company, $1.99)**- Use the modeling example on the app labeled "Waiting in Line." Have students view the app, then role play the scenario of waiting in line.
- **Living Safely (Ablelink Technologies Inc., $39.99)**- Conduct a teaching unit about safety at work. Use the app to view the content about work safety. Have students use photos or picture icons to tell three important tips to being safe at work.
- **Visual Impact (Ablelink Technologies Inc., $0.99)**- Start with the free basic version to have students review a video lesson about recycling. Start a classroom-wide or school-wide campaign to increase recycling efforts in the school.
- **I Get...People in My Community (I Get It LLC, $2.99)**- Use this app to help students identify community helpers. Personalize the app by putting the faces of those in the school community on the app for the students so that they can see faces of people they know.

Social Skills

- **Conversation Builder Teen For iPad (Mobile Ed. Tools, $29.99)**- Work on expressive communication by recording the student's response and playing it back to them. This app uses pictures of teens and young adults.
- **Language Builder for iPad (Mobile Education Tools, $9.99)**- Have students take turns describing the picture. Use pre-selected (by the teacher) picture icons to have students provide their selection. Record their selection in the app and listen to the sentence they created.
- **Preposition Builder (Mobile Education Tools, $7.99)**- Track progress students are having while learning prepositions with this app. Sit 1:1 with a student and work on this app together.
- **Manners (Conover Company, $0.99)**- Place this app in a listening area with headphones. Have a small group of students listen and watch the video on "Table Manners." In another center, highlight, the main concepts of the "Table Manners" lesson on chart paper with visual pictures to accompany the words. In the third center, set up a pretend restaurant and have students practice what they learned.
- **Hidden Curriculum for Adolescents and Adults (AAPC, $1.99)**- Take a few minutes a day to review one new skill about social skills on

this app for teens and adults. Post the newly learned skill on the board or in a social skills journal.
- **Emotions I Can Do (I Can Do Apps, Free)**- Do a warm up showing the students various pictures of people with expressive faces. Talk about the some of the emotions in the pictures. Use the app to have students take turns in the group answering the app's questions about the real life photos and the emotions on the people's faces.
- **The Social Express for iPad (The Language Express Inc. $29.99)**- Use this app as an ongoing unit on social skills instruction for teens and young adults.
- **Social Quest (Smarty Ears, $21.99)**- This app gives tips for dealing with social situations. Choose the "auditorium" section of the app and try using the app before a school wide assembly to prepare students with skills and information to get through the assembly on a positive note.
- **Social Stories (Proteon Software, $3.99)**- Customize this app to create a social story for a student who may be having difficulty with keeping an inside voice during lessons. The social story can tell the student the expected way to interact during lessons.

Recreational Skills

- **Entertainment at Home HD (Conover Company, $1.99)**- Show the video section about "cards" as a jump start to teaching recreational skills in this area. Then, play a card game with the student.
- **DC Comics (DC Entertainment, Free)**- Download and watch various comic books on the app. Some are free, some are paid. Have students create their own comic book character and story.
- **Ratatap Drums Free (Mode of Expression, LLC, Free)**- Turn on some music and let the students keep the beat with this app that lets the students tap away.
- **Lego Star Wars Funzone (The LEGO Group, Free)**- Students may find this as a great way to relax and have fun. They can watch videos, make creations or activate lightsabers with this app.
- **Monster Truck Total Destruction (Hesham Ahmed Kamal, Free)**- View some videos of monster trucks during a unit on transportation. Play the game on the app to have students see virtual monster trucks in action.
- **Monster Truck Destruction (Chillingo, Free)**- Visit the virtual car

body shop on the app and look under the hood of the car. Have students observe a real engine or real parts from under the hood of a car.
- **Talking Ben (Outfit7, Free)**- Use Ben to encourage laughs in students as they watch and listen to Ben imitate what they say. Have a set of picture cards for students to name out loud and see if Ben will imitate what they say.
- **3D Math Racing (POTG Apps, Free)**- Use race cars to learn math facts with this app. Teach skip counting with car jumps, crashes and slides.
- **Fluidity (Nebulus Design, Free)**- This app has rapid movement so be careful with using it with anyone who is prone to seizures. The app changes colors through the use of touch. It may be a relaxing app for a student during leisure time.
- **Cut the Rope HD Lite (Chillingo Ltd, Free**)- Some students may like to try this app just for fun. They have to feed the monster by cutting the rope in the correct spot.

Science/Sensory Involvement/STEM

- **Mathtopia (Omega Labs, Free)**- After a lesson related to 2-digit addition, use this app to help students practice adding two digit numbers. Students practice clearing "stamps" on the screen.
- **Bad Piggies (Rovio Entertainment, Ltd. $0.99)**- Increase physics skills and knowledge with building and racing. After playing the app, have students use wooden blocks, craft sticks and toy cars to build their own rolling or flying machine.
- **iLearn Solar System HD (Sprite Labs, $2.99)**- Use a piece of black construction paper and colored chalk to make a visual representation of the solar system. Have students use the app for reference.
- **Magic School Bus: Ocean Life (Scholastic Inc., Free)**- Show the students the "food chain" section of the app. Use a large screen projector to project the image on the wall. Use the image to begin a science discussion about food chains.
- **Kid Science (CS Web Concepts & Design LLC, $4.99)**- Follow the directions on the app to make cornstarch goo. Allow students to play with the goo for a sensory experience.
- **TikiTotems 2 (Rafal Staszewski, $0.99)**- Be engineers or construction workers as you play this game with students. Develop their engineering

skills afterwards as they play Jenga or a block stacking game.
- **Mad Math (Lunchbox Apps, $1.99)**- Create a digital flashcard program with this app as it allows you to set specific programs for each user and maintain statistics and work progress for each of them.
- **Symmetry Shuffle (Carstens Studio, Inc., $1.99)**- Sharpen spatial reasoning and geometric modeling with this app. Then, play a game related to the app using teacher-made cards.
- **Jr. Astronaut (Immediate Media Company Bristol Limited, Free)**- As a class, build a model rocket together or use shape cutouts to form a rocket picture. Use the app to practice building a rocket as well.
- **TalkCalc (Glenn Collins, Free)**- Use this fun way to visually show the functions of a calculator. Allow a student to use this TalkCalc when learning to use a calculator. The app verbally labels the keys and the answer for the user.

Social Studies (History, Geography, Politics)

- **Kids African Plains Free App (Grasshopper Apps, Free)**- Real pictures and easy puzzles are located on this app. Have students complete the puzzle on the app, then complete a teacher-made color printed "puzzle" of a laminated picture of an animal being studied.
- **Species on the Edge (Harper Collins Publishers $1.99)**- Examine the endangered animals listed in the app, then have students create their own trading cards to promote awareness about endangered animals.
- **Monte-Lingual Lite - Montessori Counting 1 to 10 (Continuous Integration Inc., Free)**- Study the Chinese New Year. Have students gain knowledge of the language by learning to count to 10 in the Mandarin language.
- **United States Spelling (Kissyface Interactive, $0.99)**- Have a spelling bee in which students match individual letter cards to the written spelled state name or match magnetic letters to the written spelled state name on a magnetic board.
- **Touchable Earth (Touchable Earth, $1.99)**- This digital book with instructions and lessons by kids 6-12 can be used as a great geography enhancement. Use it after locating a specific country on a large world map. It is filled with facts, culture, family traditions, school life and play. In-app purchases can provide more information from other countries.

- **GeoMaster Plus HD (Visuamobile, $0.99)-** Use the flag game section of this app to have students choose the correct flags of the targeted country.
- **American Presidents for iPad (Smithsonian Institution, $6.99)-** Forget heavy encyclopedia's, use this app to discover more during a unit on a famous U.S. president. See portraits and find facts. In class, have students pose for or create a "presidential style" photograph of themselves.
- **Ansel & Clair's Paul Revere's Ride (Cognitive Kid, Inc., $4.99)-** Read the book Paul Revere's Ride (Longfellow & Rand). Play the app with the students. Use 10 pre-written descriptive words and have students tell what they liked about the book and what they liked about the app. Use a large graphic organizer to visually show the differences and similarities.
- **Geo Walk HD (Vito Technology, Inc., $2.99)-** Conduct research on a variety of topics using this app. Students can scan through the app and choose a picture to learn more about or they can use the globe and pick a particular region of the world to learn more about. Try having them choose a continent and take the app quiz.
- **The Elements: A Visual Exploration (Touch Press, $13.99)-** Bring in two pieces of common elements and have the students locate the elements on the app. Read the information and view the vivid pictures to learn more about the elements.

Literacy Skills

- **United States Puzzle Map for iPad (Jenny Sun, $2.99)-** Match puzzle pieces by dragging them to the appropriate state. Afterward, play a matching game with 5 written state names.
- **Little Speller Three Letter Words LITE (GrasshopperApps.com, Free)-** Have students spell the word on the app. Next, have students make a list of 5 spelling words by asking them to write the word on paper or find the pre-made index card with the word and glue the word onto paper.
- **Educreations Interactive Whiteboard (Educreations Inc., Free)-** Upload any picture (even from the web) of your choice and add notations, text and vocabulary words on the picture with ease.
- **Sentence Builder (Mobile Education Store, LLC, $5.99)-** Write a sentence on the board and have the students practice typing on the iPad

by copying it into the app. Play the sentence back to get an audio version of the written words.
- **I Can Do Apps-Associations (I Can Do Apps, LLC, $2.99)**- Have a set of real objects (mimicking the ones on the app) to have students match "what goes together" after having them complete some associations on the app.
- **Scribblenauts Remix (Warner Bros., $0.99)**- Practice spelling with this app. Provide a list of spelling words (nouns) to the students. Use the app to practice typing the words on the iPad and see the picture pop up on the screen.
- **Rhyming Words (I Can Do Apps, Free)**- Use the app first to see picture sets of rhyming words. Then, use 3 pairs of real objects to have students choose the pairs that rhyme. Next, complete a worksheet by having students use pre-cut strips of yarn to connect the pictures on one side to the pictures that rhyme on the other side.
- **Concepts (Grasshopper Apps LLC, Free)**- With over 200 real photo examples, this app can be very motivating. Although this app can do same/different, left/right, colors, opposites and more, it can be used more specifically to increase math literacy by focusing on concepts such as sizes, length, time, before and after.
- **Phonics Genius (Innovative Mobile Apps, Free)**- An easy and great way to review or introduce sight words, customize this app to address specific long vowel sound, short vowel sounds or blends. The app allows the users to record themselves saying the word after the word is read by the iPad.
- **Abilipad (Cheryl Bregman, $19.99)**- This app can be used to download ready-made activities from the app's library. For example, the activity with "Today is ___. Tomorrow it will be _____." can be used for a morning opening activity.

Fine Motor

- **Dexteria VPP- Fine Motor Skill Development (Binary Labs, $9.99)**- Occupational Therapists will be glad to see this app. Practice finger sequencing and isolation with that section of this app.
- **iBuild ABC's (Chris Kieffer, $0.99)**- Build ABC's on the app, then have students paint wooden letters of their name or initials to use as a decorative item for their home.

- **101 Tangrams for iPad (Deitmar Schwarz Webers, $1.99)**- Have one student use a real tangram puzzle to practice creating images with the pieces, then have another student use the app while waiting for the real puzzle. After a few minutes, switch.
- **Etch-a-scketch for iPad (Freeze Tag, Inc., $2.99)**- Have fun with this app after a unit on geometry to have students draw lines to make various shapes.
- **Ready to Print for iPad (Essare, $9.99)**- This app has a lot to offer such as pre-writing skills, shapes, tracing, matching, connect the dots, pinching movements, forming letters, forming numbers and more. Use it to have students draw geometric shapes during a geometry lesson.
- **Drawnimal (Lucas Zanotto, $1.99)**- Draw funny animals using a pencil and paper that is placed under the iPad. The app encourages you to expand the creative space of the iPad by putting paper under it and drawing the creation around the iPad and around the picture on the iPad.
- **Powerful Printing (Write On Handwriting, $2.99)**- Work on specific initial pencil strokes for those needing assistance in this area.
- **Talking Roby Celik the Robot for iPad (Outfit7, Free)**- Have students build sentences with pre-written word cards on a sentence strip or on paper. Have students type in (give assistance when needed) the sentence onto the robot's screen. Listen to the robot repeat what is typed.
- **P.O.V.-Spatial Reasoning Skills Development (Binary Labs, $2.99)**- Use this app with students who many seem to have a difficult time with judging space and time. The activities in this app help to develop spatial reasoning skills.
- **Stack the States (Dan Russell-Pinson, Free)**- Play the app and answer the questions about each state. Then have fun using an isolated pointer finger to drop the state into a stacked pile.

Physical Education

- **C-Fit XTrain (Classroom Fitness, $0.99)**- Review the vocabulary words in the app before having students use it. Have the students act them out to show understanding of the definitions. Use the app to do a workout as a class.
- **C-Fit Yoga (Classroom Fitness, $0.99)**- Help students learn calming and relaxing techniques through this app. Choose 2 poses to have

students practice each morning before completing work tasks.
- **Glow Hockey 2 for iPad Free (Natenai Ariyatrakool, Free)**- Divide the students into groups. Have one group work in the play area using a real hockey puck and hockey stick, the second group at a small table learning the vocabulary terms about hockey and the third group taking turns using the glow hockey app.
- **Cardiograph (MacroPinch Ltd., $1.99)**- In Health class, have students place pictures of a heart onto the correct position on a picture of a person. Talk about the role of the heart. Use the app with the class to practice measuring the heart rates of each student.
- **Smash Your Food HD** (**Food N' Me, $2.99**)- Use this during a health lesson to help kids realize how much sugar, salt and oil is in the foods they eat. Pick 4 foods they can create on the app and then have them "smash" the food away. They can actually hear every squish, glop, fizz and pop!
- **Chop Chop Tennis HD (Gamerizon, $0.99)**- Teach the students how to serve a tennis ball. Use the game app to practice a full game.
- **Kurt Warner's Football 101 for Kids (Good Sports Gang LLC, $2.99**)- This app provides the basics of football to beginners. Use this app along with the students first, then take students out to the field to practice one or two skills.
- **BurstMode (Cogitap, $1.99)**- You can capture sports, skateboard tricks or any fast action where the action occurs quickly. Try using this app to make a video model of how to play a specific sport or how to make a specific sports move. Play it back to the students in slow motion.
- **Flick Golf! Free (Full Fat, Free)**- This app can be used before a class trip to play mini-golf at a mini-golf activity center.
- **Action Bowling HD (Kronos Games, Free)**- Have fun with virtual bowling. Teach vocabulary related to bowling such as strike and spare. Keep a written sight word card of each word on the board. Then have students use the terms during the game.

Notes:

Resources

Books:

Linton, S. B. (2012). How to Set Up a Classroom For Students with Autism Second Edition: A Manual for Teachers, Para-professionals and Administrators AutismClassroom.com.

Linton, S. B. (2010). Lesson Ideas and Activities for Young Children with Autism and Related Special Needs: Activities, Apps & Lessons for Joint Attention, Imitation, Play, Social Skills & More. AutismClassroom.com.

Websites:

www.autismclassroom.com

www.corestandards.org

www.apple.com/itunes

About the Author

S. B. Linton has worked with children with autism for over 15 years. She has a Master's Degree in Teaching Students with Severe Disabilities and a Graduate Certificate in Autism Spectrum Disorders from Johns Hopkins University. Linton is the also the author of the books *How to Set Up a Classroom for Students with Autism Second Edition, How to Set Up a Work Area at Home for a Child with Autism* and *Lesson Ideas and Activities for Young Children with Autism and Related Special Needs: Activities, Apps & Lessons for Joint Attention, Imitation, Play, Social Skills & More*. She is the creator of the apps *Autism At Home, Autism Classroom, Teens with Autism* and *Room Layout*. She currently works as an Autism Instructional Specialist and consults with school teams in matters related to teaching students with autism.

Made in the USA
Lexington, KY
04 September 2013